Striking Back

Post Stroke Poetry

Eric Barr

ARROYO SECO PRESS

Logo by Morgan G Robles

Arroyo Seco Press

www.arroyosecopress.org

Cover art: by Willfried Wende from Pixabay

ISBN: 979-8-9918724-5-4

To my wife Karen, friends, family, and the pets and poets that helped to bring me back to life after my stroke. You all inspired and continue to inspire me to live fully and to write. Love to all.

Poems

On visiting my dying friend.

Yesterday
I visited my dying friend
That's good
Tomorrow
would've been
One day
 too late.

Once I was the skinny one to his muscular, brawny frame,
But dying had diminished him.
Now he was the skinny one,
skeletal with a flesh shroud

I talked to him
He did not respond.
I don't know if he heard me, but I talked.

Most of the visit his eyes were closed
So, I don't think he saw me.
No looking, no talking,

Maybe he was practicing being dead.
Or just communing with those who already were.

Sitting near him on the bed,
I tried to understand his groans and mumblings.
His wit and words were gone, all that remained
Was sound.

The sound of labored breath
His once flat stomach was bloated with illness
And his arms that could chop and carry wood,
Could hardly lift him out of a chair.

Dying had already taken so much of him,
There was little left for death to take.

Old Guys Talking

I am at the age where
Every conversation turns into a discussion
Of Doctors, surgeries, & medications
I am also at the point where I don't
Bother with the pleasantries
I'm happy to start with the kid at
The hardware store by saying

"I need a nightlight, I'm up all night
Peeing and I'm gonna kill myself
Getting to the toilet.
Someday your prostate will
Squeeze your urethra like
A vice lock pliers."

"Hey kid I bet you still wake up with a hard on."

I used to have other things to talk about;
Interesting things, ideas, concepts
Hopes and dreams.
Now I just hope I can remember who I am,
And I dream about the time when my body worked.

At least discussing healthcare beats talking politics
Even if I agree with you,

I'd rather hear what your doctor said about your hemorrhoidectomy
Than listen to you regurgitating what you think you heard on the news.

mornings

I start each day
Sitting at the front window
Staring down the driveway
Hoping the past or future will
Ride up, on the lone Ranger's white horse and visit,
But I end up sitting alone
Me with my coffee
The dog with her bone.
What could the past tell me
What would I like the future to say,
You didn't screw up too badly
At least you've got today.

When all is said and done

When all is said and done
comes much too soon.
Some days are so short,
I have to talk in my sleep and run in my dreams
Just to keep up.

The days too short
The years too few
There's nothing
 to do

But

Walk the dog
Stay close to your friends
And move wildly to little Richard's music.

Time is
Running

Out.

On the Run

Here we run from fires,
conflagrations
There they run from the unrelenting rain
Some people run from true love
Others run from the fear of pain

Some run from what's over and done
While others hide from what's yet to come
With enough warning
I can outrun trouble

But what I,
and most of us,
Can't get away from

Is the less than
Whole
person
I have,
we will,
become.

Flammable

Smoke from
Canadian wildfires
Blankets the Midwest
Mojave wildfires
Shroud
Palm Springs
Even worse
D.C.'s stench
Chokes the country

Most wildfires
And all
Political corruption
Are man made
Both destroy lives
And spread like the
Measles.

I am old   and cranky
and the
Earth is suffering
From all
     The shit
We've done to
Her.

Heat waves bake the west
Torrential rains flood Texas
Tornadoes tear up the Midwest
Wars are spreading across the globe
The polar caps are melting.

People can't be
Civil
To each other
Nothing is
As
It should be

I stopped listening
To the news
Now I
Can't even listen to the weather

Paper

The only thing
You can count on is
Paper

All
The   Kleenex boxes
In The house
Run out at the
Same time
Likewise
All the Charmin
Comes off
The cardboard rolls
In every bathroom
In the house
On the same day.

The printer runs out of
Paper
When you need
It
The most.

Everything is
Connected.

And
Everything is flammable

The missing and the dead

I long to talk
to the dead
and
The missing.

I have so many questions
And something
To tell them

It's important
To me
But probably won't mean much
To them

Do you ever wonder
What happened to me?

Are they listening?
Would they even care?
And if they were
And did.

How could I explain my
Life to them?

I am not the person
They knew
And they must have
Changed too
Little by little
As we do.

When I used to think of you
It made me smile
Now
thinking
of you
Only reminds
me
That
everyone
can and will
Disappear.

Them and Me

My wife's friend is a queen of chaos.
She travels in a cloud of pandemonium,
It surrounds her like
The heavy scent of perfume that
envelopes many elderly women.

Like these ladies, who liberally splash perfume,
This woman willingly wraps
Herself in bedlam.

Too many cars and too many homes,
Don't provide a cushion
or the aura of success,
They just multiply the
Opportunities for a mess.

I guess this is what's meant by too much
Of a good thing

When he was alive
My friend was another person who thrived on chaos.
He was always surrounded by mayhem,
(of his own making)
Which he willingly stepped into
And wore proudly like his
Cowboy finery

he had too many animals and vehicles,
Which meant that some animal was always sick or lost
And at least one vehicle was broken down and up on blocks.

In his day, this man
could build things,
He
could do plumbing and electrical work;
But in keeping with his need for disorder,
He assembled things backwards on purpose.
So only
he could fix them.

Unfortunately, he usually forgot this personal touch.

So, when something stopped working,
He was surprised often shocked to find negative where positive should be.

When he was dying you could almost see the chaos falling away from him
But like his spirit, it was strong and not easily lost.
Even in his final hours he was crawling under the rented hospital bed,
Rewiring it backwards.
Then we had to move the bed to set him free,
So, one day later he could escape his earthly bonds
I want to believe that now dead he is at peace
But I can't be sure
For both of these people the need for disorder was as essential as oxygen.

And I suppose I needed and wanted them both in my life
I got some excitement from their chaos.
I got caught up and participated in it
Even though it interrupted the
calmness and acceptable disorder of my existence.

My friend who is living, but not very happily,
Is an artist of anxiety.
Instead of blending yellow, blue, and red,
He mixes worry, guilt, and dread
Turning everyday challenges into
Complex, pointillistic puzzles.
He doesn't just complain,
He whines.
You can even hear the whining in his emails

It bothers me to see myself in his dysfunctions.
But I need and enjoy his company.
If only to help me see my own craziness
And feel better about it.

I don't want the extra madness and chaos in my life
But I guess I like it around the edges, in the periphery,
Behind me
Where it creates excitement without dragging me in too deep

I just need to remember what we all learned in Driver's Education
Objects in mirror are closer than they appear.

The New Normal

A phrase no doubt created
By a consultant or mid-level
Asshole

Everything is fucked up
And it's not going to get better

What should we tell the employees?
Don't worry, this is the new normal.

No one ever says
You won the lottery
    Now you're filthy rich
  This is your new normal

Or the cancer is gone.
  Healthy is your new normal.

Nope
The new normal is   used to make bad news
Sound like
You
Can
Live with it.

Waiting for the Doctor

Just being here
I feel better already.
I'm sure it's nothing.

He'll say, "Cut down the bourbon
And get more exercise."

The walls are pale blue,
The carpet unobtrusive
Even the doctor is almost invisible

The diplomas on the wall
Tell me this guy
"Knows his stuff.

But, The skeleton in the corner
Says, "Doesn't matter.
      You'll look just like me
      soon enough".

Sunset Walk

On tonight's unsteady sunset walk
The crows squawked,
the crickets chirped,
and even
the blue birds
were screaming at me
to fall and die.
To provide a bigger meal
than the roadkill rabbit
at the end of the drive.

An ICU Room must be a miserable place to die

Two blank monitors staring at you
Black doorways to eternity.

And a third one showing you your inner workings
in colorful lines and mechanical beeps
A white board with today's date
Look how far you made it.
A Clock ticking off the seconds left
The nurses moving constantly to keep you alive
Their smiles and energy high
To keep you upbeat.

On the wall, a bad still life of flowers in a vase
To be viewed by the stilled life in the bed
Three boxes of rubber gloves
So, everyone, no matter their size
Can Get their hands on you
To take your blood and dignity.
The monitors ringing all night

For whom the bells toll?
no surprise, it's for you.
The blood pressure cuff squeezing you awake at night
Like a friend grabbing your arm with a secret
But there is no secret.
This is where people come to make their final exits.

Never before has the thought of
Dying at home been so comforting.

Sleeping Arrangements

Since my stroke
The dog sleeps in bed with my wife and me.
We each have our place in bed
And the dog is always the first one in.
She circles and curls near the foot of the bed
Until I am in my Hand and Foot Splints
And my CPAP mask.
Then she lies beside me and rests
Her head on my once paralyzed leg.

I love when she sleeps like that
It reminds me I am not
sleeping in a hospital bed or
Lying in a casket

Even better,
when she dreams and runs in her sleep
It wakes me so I can enjoy the warmth of the blanket
And the cover of dark.
Then we both fall asleep
And back into our dreams of Running

Some days
I wake Opie from her nap,
Pet her with my unsplinted hand
Just to assure myself
I'm not living in a nursing home.

Even though
It has been eight years since
I was in the hospital or the rehab center.

Those places have a hold on my brain
The way a squirrel on the porch
Holds my dog's attention

Who Will Die First?

That's a question
I ask about
       My family
        My friends
         My pets.

It's not that I think about death a lot.
Like most people I don't notice that
I'm alive.

Until there is something to complain about.
Aye, there's the rub.
We're barely aware that we're alive.

Some days, I don't notice

the taste of the
         orange juice
The sun
        on my back,
The breeze
        in my face.

We are just
So busy
being and doing every day.
That we don't notice being alive until it is almost
Too late.

Maybe the question should be

Who will taste the orange juice first?

Up On the Roof

When my medications make me feel like jumping off a roof
I Can't tell the difference between my emotions and the medications

How do I convince myself that it is
The meds not me?
That my feelings are a chemical reaction.
Not a true self-reflection

In time, after conversations with my wife, friends, and dog
I am able to distinguish my feelings from those generated by the drugs.
And I talk myself down

"Stay off the roof, stay off the roof." I tell myself as I lie in bed
   under a cover.
When I realize a fall from the roof
will only make things worse
and require more drugs
I settle down with the dog,
We Fall asleep,

and dream of flying.

Birds fly Rocks Fall

Sometimes while chasing
a luscious bug to eat
Or blinded by the reflection of the sun
A bird will accidentally fly into the
Living room picture window

It floats to the porch
Unconscious
Or dead
With a delicate thud.

How many times have I
Been stopped cold
Chasing something
I want right now
Blinded by beauty, by the flesh
Only to crash into an invisible force
Right in front of me

And my fall is loud
As elbows, knees, and head bounce on the
Ground
I still have the bruises.

Who among us has not run into
unforeseen consequences
Or a rock-solid conscience
During a pursuit
When blinded by a Promise,
Blinded by desires, hopes, or dreams.

I Know that pursuing my desires can be dangerous.

But never pursuing anything
Would break my spirit.

Whole

To be able to use
    Both hands
To
    WASH THE DISHES.
To be able to walk
Without having
To think about
    How to walk.

Since my stroke
Twelve years ago
I have been hemipelagic,
My left arm and left leg
Were left paralyzed.
Meaning that medically
I am considered
    Half
Not
    Whole

Oh, to be Whole again
But in losing the use of my arm and leg
I have grown one appendage for
    Compassion
And another for
    Empathy

Although, because the stroke altered how
    I speak.
    I sound
    Gruff, short, and angry
To others

Despite being only
    Half.
I like
    And treat
Myself and others
    A whole
Lot
Better than
I did before
When I really was
    Whole.

Acknowledgements

These poems were previously published in these publications:

On Visiting My Dying Friend – *California's Best Emerging Poets 2020: An Anthology*, & *Z Publishing House*

ICU Room Must be a Miserable place to Die – *The Journal of Radical Wonder* Sept 17, 2023

Sleeping Arrangements – *The Journal Of Radical Wonder* May 22, 2023

Birds fly , Rocks Fall – *Sheila Na Gig* Volume 9.3 Spring 2025

Whole, **Sunset Walk** & **Up On The Roof** – *Synchronized Chaos* May 5, 2025

Biography

Eric Barr taught acting and directing at University of California, Riverside from 1975 until 2013. He was the Chairman of the UCR Theatre Department for over 30 years and the Founding Director of the UCR Palm Desert MFA in Creative Writing and Writing for the Performing Arts.

 Barr was a has written screenplays, plays, essays and three of his short stories have appeared in *Connotation Press* In addition to his writing, Eric has worked as a theatre director and acting coach; He was the Artistic Director of the Porthouse Theatre in Cleveland, taught movement for actors at the Stella Adler Conservatory of Acting in Los Angeles, and worked as an acting coach with the National Theatre of the Deaf.

Since surviving a series of strokes Barr has written a one-man show, *A Piece of my Mind*, about his surgeries, hospitalizations, and rehab, that he performs, around the country, for hospitals, med schools, stroke associations, and general theatre audiences. His podcasts on stroke recovery, video of his one man show, and documentary can be found at www.apieceofmymind.net

In 2020, Barr began to write poetry to help his memory which was damaged by his strokes eight years earlier. His first poem *On Visiting My Dying Friend* was published in the collection California's Best Emerging Poets of 2020. Three other poems were published in *The Journal of Radical Wonder*.

www.ingramcontent.com/pod-product-compliance
Lightning Source LLC
Chambersburg PA
CBHW072020060426
42446CB00044B/3218